The Last Soldiers of the Son

An Expose Against Islam

Authored by

Dr. Andrew Ho, MD, PhD

Dr. Samuel Samson

www.thelastsoldiers.com

ATP, LLC   Denver, CO

Printed in the United States of America

ISBN: 1453762256

This work is dedicated to

the last martyrs of the Son

Table of Contents

Forward to the End

Andrew Ho, MD, PhD

Religion is derived from the Latin root *religare* which means to "bind fast". And we are all bound fast to that which we hold to be true. For we as God's children are bondservants of the true and living God. And we as His bondservants are to preach the words of Christ our Lord. "For we do not preach ourselves, but Christ Jesus the Lord, and ourselves your **bondservants** for Jesus' sake. For it is the God who commanded light to shine out of darkness, who has shone in our hearts to give the light of the knowledge of the glory of God in the face of Jesus Christ." (2 Corinthians 4:5-6)   And by speaking the words of Christ, we speak His words of truth. For as He said, "I am the way, the truth, and the life. No one comes to the Father except through Me." (John 14:6)

And Islam claims that they serve God. And although they may truly love God, they too shall be bound to that which they hold to be true. And the authors of this book, being bondservants of God, are commanded to speak the truth. And the truth is this, that Islam does not speak the truth, for the foundation of this religion is based upon a lie. And by being a lie, the father of Islam is Satan, for Satan is the father of all lies. As is said, "you belong to your father, the devil, and you want to carry out your father's desire. He was a murderer from the beginning, not holding to the truth, for there is no truth in him. When he *lies*, he speaks his native language, for he is a *liar* and the father of *lies*." (John 8:44)

And Mohammed, the father of Islam, was a liar. For as we shall see, Islam was based upon a great lie, for he was not bound to the true and living God. And by being a liar, he was a bondservant of the father of all lies who is Satan. And the fate of all liars is death. For as the prophecy says, "but the cowardly, the unbelieving, the vile, the murderers, the sexually immoral, those who practice magic arts, the idolaters and all *liars*--their place will be in the fiery lake of burning sulfur. This is the second death." (Revelation 21:8)

And Mohammed was a false prophet. For prophecy means to know the will of God. For he did not know the will of God, but the will of an idol and of Satan. And the fate of all false prophets is eternal death. "So My hand will be against the *prophets* who see *false* visions and utter lying divinations. They will have no place in the council of My people, nor will they be written down in the register of the house of Israel, nor will they enter the land of Israel, that you may know that I am the Lord God." (Ezekiel 13:9)

And although Muslims may truly love God, they shall be bound to that which they follow. For by following a religion that is based on a lie, they shall follow its father who is Satan. And by following the father of Islam, they follow Mohammed, a liar and a false prophet. And at the end, the beast who is Satan, and the false prophet, who is Mohammed, shall be thrown into the lake fire. For as the prophecy says, "the *beast* was seized, and with him the *false prophet* who performed the signs in his presence, by which he deceived those who had received the mark of the *beast* and those who worshiped his image; these two were thrown alive into the lake of fire which burns with brimstone." (Revelation 19:20) And by following Islam, their followers must be killed by the sword, and devoured by the beasts of the field. "And the rest were killed with the sword which came from the mouth of Him who sat on the horse, and all the birds were filled with their flesh." (Revelation 19:21)

But there is still hope, for many will turn to the Son at his second coming. And our hope is that many in Islam, will come to know the true and living God. For the true and living God is the Son, and through the Son we know the Father, and through the Father and the Son we receive the Holy Spirit. And at the end by knowing the Son, we shall inherit eternal life. For "we know that the Son of God has come and has given us an understanding, that we may know Him who is true; and we are in Him who is true, in His Son Jesus Christ. This is the true God and eternal life." (1 John 5:20) And at the end, though we may die, we shall enter the heavens and be made alive. For as the prophecy says, "for as in Adam all die, so also in Christ all will be made alive. But each in his own order: Christ the first fruits, after that those who are Christ's at His coming." (1 Corinthians 15:22-23) But to those who remain, they shall be subject to God's judgment, which is death. For as the prophecy ends, "then comes the end, when He delivers the kingdom to God the Father, when He puts an end to all rule and all authority and power. For He must reign till He has put all enemies under His feet. The last enemy that will be destroyed *is* death. For *"He has put all things under His feet."* (1 Corinthians 15:24-27)

Are You With Him Or Against Him?

Andrew Ho, PhD, MD

"Behold, away from the fertility of the earth shall be your dwelling, and away from the dew of heaven from above. By your sword you shall live, and your brother you shall serve; but it shall come about when you become restless, that you will break his yoke from your neck." (Genesis 27:39-40) For the time is at hand, when Esau shall break the yoke that has been placed around his neck. For the nations of Islam have been withheld from the fertility of the earth, for they have been held from the dew of the heavens above. And they have been subject to the trials and tribulations of this earth, even to this day. But we as God's people have inherited His blessings. And as the Son has been faithful to us, so should we be faithful to Him. For as He asks of every man, will you stand with Me? For "He who is not with Me is against Me". (Matthew 12:30)

For the yoke of Esau has been carried through the blood of Islam. And Islam is derived from the Arabic word *istislam* which means "in submission to the will of Allah". But as we know, all things are not subject to Allah, but to the will of YHWH, who is God. And we as brothers and sisters of the Son, and we as children of the Father, have followed His commands, even to this day. For as He said, "behold My mother and My brothers! For whoever does the will of God, he is My brother and sister and mother." (Mark 3:34-35) And the nations of Islam have been subject to the will of the Father. For as the Father said of the descendants of Ishmael, "he will be a wild donkey of a man, his hand will be against everyone, and everyone's hand will be against him; and he will live to the east of all his brothers." (Genesis 16:12) And "they settled from Havilah to Shur which is east of Egypt as one goes toward Assyria; he settled in defiance of all his relatives." (Genesis 25:18) And the nations of Islam have pulled the yoke as was foretold. But they have been at enmity with the nations of the land. For in defiance of the Father, brother wars against brother, even to this day.

And the nations of Islam and Judaism have followed the will of the Father. For as the Father said to the mother of Esau and Jacob, "two nations are in your womb; and two peoples will be separated from your body; and one people shall be stronger than the other; and the older shall serve the younger." (Genesis 25:23) And the nations of Islam continue to serve the nations of Judaism, even to this day.

But the fruit of Judaism was wrought through deceit. For the inheritance of Jacob was conceived through a lie. And through this deceitful lie, Jacob would receive the blessings of the firstborn, the inheritance of Esau. "See, the smell of my son is like the smell of a field which the Lord has blessed; now may God give you of the dew of heaven, and of the fatness of the earth, and an abundance of grain and new wine; may peoples serve you, and nations bow down to you; be master of your brothers, and may your mother's sons bow down to you. Cursed be those who curse you, and blessed be those who bless you." (Genesis 27:27-29) And Islam continues to serve Judaism, even to this day.

And the curse of Islam was wrought through denial. For the curse of Islam was conceived, by Esau forsaking his birthright for some stew. "For Jacob said, 'First swear to me'; so he swore to him, and sold his birthright to Jacob. Then Jacob gave Esau bread and lentil stew; and he ate and drank, and rose and went on his way. Thus Esau despised his birthright." (Genesis 25:33-34) And by Esau forsaking his birthright, he would be cursed by this inheritance. "Behold, away from the fertility of the earth shall be your dwelling, and away from the dew of heaven from above. By your sword you shall live, and your brother you shall serve; but it shall come about when you become restless, that you will break his yoke from your neck." (Genesis 27:39-40) And Islam continues to serve his brother, even to this day. But the yoke shall be broken, for the nations are restless, and the end is near.

For the plow has been pulled by the donkey of Islam, but has been let slack by the oxen of Israel. And both have forsaken the commands of the Father, for as the Father had commanded His people, "you shall not plow with an ox and a donkey together." (Deuteronomy 22:10) And in God's justice, both nations shall be destroyed. For "your ox shall be slaughtered before your eyes, but you will not eat of it; your donkey shall be torn away from you, and will not be restored to you." (Deuteronomy 28:31)

And the only righteous promise has come through the Son. For only the Son has remained steadfast to the Father. For as the Son testified, "truly, truly, I say to you, the Son can do nothing of Himself, unless it is something He sees the Father doing; for whatever the Father does, these things the Son also does in like manner." (John 5:19) And it is only through the Son, that we can receive the promises of the Father. For as the Son said "all things have been handed over to Me by My Father, and no one knows who the Son is except the Father, and who the Father is except the Son, and anyone to whom the Son wills to reveal Him." (Luke 10:22) And the promise from the Father and the Son is eternal life. For "the Father loves the Son and has given all things into His hand. He who believes in the Son has eternal life". (John 3:36) But to deny the Son is to be subject to the wrath of God. For "he who does not obey the Son will not see life, but the wrath of God abides on him." (John 3:36)

And truly, time has held these promises true. And to believe in the Son is to deny oneself, even unto death. For as the Son said, "if anyone wishes to come after Me, he must deny himself, and take up his cross daily and follow Me." And the reward of denying oneself is to gain eternal life. But to deny the Son is to lose one's life. For "whoever wishes to save his life will lose it, but whoever loses his life for My sake, he is the one who will save it. For what is a man profited if he gains the whole world, and loses or forfeits himself? For whoever is ashamed of Me and My words, the Son of Man will be ashamed of him when He comes in His glory, and the glory of the Father and of the holy angels. But I say to you truthfully, there are some of those standing here who will not taste death until they see the kingdom of God." (Luke 9:23-27)

And as the day approaches, many shall assume the mark of the beast. For to deny the Son of Man, and to deny that He is God, is to assume the mark of the beast. For as the Son said of the beast, "any kingdom divided against itself is laid waste; and any city or house divided against itself will not stand. If I by Beelzebul cast out demons, by whom do your sons cast them out? For this reason they will be your judges. But if I cast out demons by the Spirit of God, then the kingdom of God has come upon you. Or how can anyone enter the strong man's house and carry off his property, unless he first binds the strong man? And then he will plunder his house. He who is not with Me is against Me; and he who does not gather with Me scatters." (Matthew 12:26-30)   And those who follow Mohammad have followed the false prophet. For as we shall see, his words have been wrought not by the truth, but by malice and lies. And those who assume the mark of the beast, and those who follow the false prophet, they shall be subject to the judgment of God. For as the prophecy says, "and the beast was seized, and with him the false prophet who performed the signs in his presence, by which he deceived those who had received the mark of the beast and those who worshiped his image; these two were thrown alive into the lake of fire which burns with brimstone. And the rest were killed with the sword which came from the mouth of Him who sat on the horse, and all the birds were filled with their flesh." (Revelation 19:20-21)

He who has ears, let him hear.

Islam's Woeful Ways

Andrew Ho, PhD, MD

"Behold, I am coming quickly, and My reward is with Me, to render to every man according to what he has done. I am the Alpha and the Omega, the first and the last, the beginning and the end." (Revelation 22:12-13) And from the beginning, the blessing and the curse were established. And from the beginning, the consequences were established by the Law. For as the Father instructed His people through Moses, "See, I am setting before you today a blessing and a curse: the blessing, if you listen to the commandments of the Lord your God, which I am commanding you today; and the curse, if you do not listen to the commandments of the Lord your God, but turn aside from the way which I am commanding you today, by following other gods which you have not known." (Deuteronomy 11:26-28) And through the Son, the blessing and curse were enforced. For as He said, "Do not think that I came to abolish the Law or the Prophets; I did not come to abolish but to fulfill. For truly I say to you, until heaven and earth pass away, not the smallest letter or stroke shall pass from the Law until all is accomplished." (Matthew 5:17-18)

And what is the Law? For it was established at the

beginning, through His witness and the prophet Moses. "Hear, O Israel! The Lord is our God, the Lord is one! You shall *love* the Lord your God with all your heart and with all your soul and with all your might." (Deuteronomy 6:4) And second one is like it, "You shall not take vengeance, nor bear any grudge against the sons of your people, but you shall *love* your neighbor as yourself; I am the Lord." (Leviticus 19:18) For this Law is the sign of the Father. "You shall bind them as a sign on your hand and they shall be as frontals on your forehead." (Deuteronomy 6:8)   And the Law was reinforced by the Son.   For as the Pharisees asked Him, "Teacher, which is the great commandment in the law?" Jesus said to him, "'You shall *love* the Lord your God with all your heart, with all your soul, and with all your mind.' This is the first and great commandment. And the second is like it: 'You shall *love* your neighbor as yourself.' On these two commandments hang all the Law and the Prophets." (Matthew 22:36-40)

And as we shall see, Islam despises the Law which the Father established, and the Law which the Son gave His life to enforce. For God's Law is a Law of *compassion*. For as the Son chided His adversaries, "It is not those who are healthy who need a physician, but those who are sick. But go and learn what this means: 'I desire *compassion*, and not sacrifice,' for I did not come to call the righteous, but sinners." (Matthew 9:12-13)

8

And the Son had great compassion for His people they were like sheep without a Shepherd. "When Jesus went ashore, He saw a large crowd, and He felt *compassion* for them because they were like sheep without a shepherd; and He began to teach them many things." (Mark 6:34)

But the instruction of Islam despises God's Law of compassion. For Islam instructs that men should be fought against until Islam reigns supreme. And "fight against them until idolatry is no more and Allah's religion reigns supreme." (Quran Surat 2:193/8:39) And Islam commands that all unbelievers should be killed and beheaded. For "when you meet the unbelievers in the battlefield, strike off their heads, and when you have laid them low, bind your captives firmly." (Quran Surat 47:4) And contrary to what Muslims maintain, Jews and Christians are considered unjust, and remain at enmity with Islam. "O believers, take not Jews and Christians as friends; they are friends of each other. Those of you who make them his friends is one of them. God does not guide an unjust people." (Quran Surat 5:54) And Muslims are encouraged to fight to sustain their idolatrous cause. "Let those fight in the cause of God who sell the life of this world for the hereafter. To him who fights in the cause of God, whether he is slain or victorious, soon we shall give him a great reward." (Quran Surat 4:74)

But the Law of the Father is contrary, to Islam's woeful ways. For we as His children are encouraged to pray, for those who are at enmity with God. For as we were instructed, "I say to you who hear, *love* your enemies, do good to those who hate you, bless those who curse you, pray for those who mistreat you. Whoever hits you on the cheek, offer him the other also; and whoever takes away your coat , do not withhold your shirt from him either. Give to everyone who asks of you, and whoever takes away what is yours, do not demand it back. Treat others the same way you want them to treat you. If you *love* those who *love* you, what credit is that to you? For even sinners love those who *love* them. If you do good to those who do good to you, what credit is that to you? For even sinners do the same. If you lend to those from whom you expect to receive, what credit is that to you? Even sinners lend to sinners in order to receive back the same amount." For we have been created in the image of the Father. And we as His children are to love and show mercy, to those who despise us. "*Love* your enemies, and do good, and lend, expecting nothing in return; and your reward will be great, and you will be sons of the Most High; for He Himself is kind to ungrateful and evil men. Be merciful, just as your Father is merciful." (Luke 6:27-36)

And each man shall be judged by the law which he follows. For Islam shall be judged by its law of anger and hatred. "Therefore as I live," declares the Lord

God, "I will deal with you according to your anger and according to your envy which you showed because of your hatred against them; so I will make Myself known among them when I judge you." (Ezekiel 35:11) But we shall be judged by God's law of compassion. "Therefore the Lord longs to be gracious to you, and therefore He waits on high to have *compassion* on you. For the Lord is a God of justice; How blessed are all those who long for Him." (Isaiah 30:18)

I will make all My goodness pass before you, and I will proclaim the name of the Lord before you. I will be gracious to whom I will be gracious, and I will have compassion on whom I will have compassion.

Exodus 33:19

11

The Reward Or The Judgment?

Andrew Ho, MD, PhD

"And the nations were enraged, and Your wrath came, and the time came for the dead to be *judged*, and the time to *reward* Your bond-servants the prophets and the saints and those who fear Your name, the small and the great, and to destroy those who destroy the earth." (Revelation 11:18) And the time has come when the harvest shall be reaped. And those who have been faithful to His Word, they shall receive eternal riches. But to those who have forsaken God, they shall be subject to God's judgment. And the followers of Islam shall be subject to God's judgment, for this is what the prophecy foretold. ""I have loved you," says the Lord. But you say, "How have You loved us?" "Was not Esau Jacob's brother?" declares the Lord. "Yet I have loved Jacob; but I have hated Esau, and I have made his mountains a desolation and appointed his inheritance for the jackals of the wilderness." Though Edom says, "We have been beaten down, but we will return and build up the ruins"; thus says the Lord of hosts, "They may build, but I will tear down; and men will call them the wicked territory, and the people toward whom the Lord is indignant forever. Your eyes will see this and you will say, "The Lord be magnified beyond the border of Israel!"" (Malachi 1:1-5)

And the children of God shall receive eternal riches. For by the Son's power, we shall be made alive. "For as in Adam all die, so also in Christ all will be made alive. But each in his own order: Christ the first fruits, after that those who are Christ's at His coming." (1 Corinthians 15:22-23) But the followers of Islam, they are the enemies the Son shall defeat. For as the verse continues, "then comes the end, when He hands over the kingdom to the God and Father, when He has abolished all rule and all authority and power. For He must reign until He has put all His enemies under His feet." (1 Corinthians 15:24-25)

And the Son Himself shall raise us up on that day. "For this is the will of My Father, that everyone who beholds the Son and believes in Him will have eternal life, and I Myself will raise him up on the last day." (John 6:40) And He shall betroth us with eternal rewards. For "behold, I am coming quickly, and My reward is with Me, to render to every man according to what he has done. I am the Alpha and the Omega, the first and the last, the beginning and the end." (Revelation 22:12-13)

But to follow the Son comes at great cost. For "as it is written: "For Your sake we are killed all day long; We are accounted as sheep for the slaughter."" But the Son shall keep up safe, even at the darkest hour. For "in all these things we are more than conquerors through Him who loved us. For I am persuaded that neither death nor life, nor angels nor principalities nor powers, nor things present nor things to come, nor height nor depth, nor any other created thing, shall be able to separate us from the love of God which is in Christ Jesus our Lord." (Romans 8:36-39) And by the sword of Islam, many shall perish before the Son returns. For the fifth seal has been opened, and the 144,000 are to be sealed. "And there was given to each of them a white robe; and they were told that they should rest for a little while longer, until the number of their fellow servants and their brethren who were to be killed even as they had been, would be completed also." (Revelation 6:11) Thus many more servants remain to be killed, before the Son returns on that day.

But the cost of forsaking the Son, comes at a much greater cost. For as the Son warned us, "whoever denies Me before men, I will also deny him before My Father who is in heaven." (Matthew 10:33) Thus each servant of Christ, must be willing to take up his cross. But "he who does not take his cross and follow after Me is not worthy of Me. He who has found his life will lose it, and he who has lost his life for My sake will find it." (Matthew 10:38-39)

And on that day, many shall choose to follow the Lamb. For *one third* of mankind shall follow the Lamb. For at the tribulation, one third of the earth shall be destroyed. And one third of mankind shall perish, in the blood of the Lamb. As the prophecy says, "and the four angels, who had been prepared for the hour and day and month and year, were released, so that they would kill a *third* of mankind." (Revelation 9:14-15) And when the four angels sound their trumpets: "the first sounded, and there came hail and fire, mixed with blood, and they were thrown to the earth; and a *third* of the earth was burned up, and a *third* of the trees were burned up, and all the green grass was burned up. The second angel sounded, and something like a great mountain burning with fire was thrown into the sea; and a *third* of the sea became blood, and a *third* of the creatures which were in the sea and had life, died; and a *third* of the ships were destroyed. The third angel sounded, and a great star fell from heaven, burning like a torch, and it fell on a *third* of the rivers and on the springs of waters. The name of the star is called Wormwood; and a *third* of the waters became wormwood, and many men died from the waters, because they were made bitter. The fourth angel sounded, and a *third* of the sun and a *third* of the moon and a *third* of the stars were struck, so that a *third* of them would be darkened and the day would not shine for a *third* of it, and the night in the same way." (Revelation 8:7-12)

And after their deaths, one third of mankind shall enter the heavens, to follow the Lamb. "And after these things I looked, and behold, a great multitude which no one could count, from every nation and all tribes and peoples and tongues, standing before the throne and before the Lamb, clothed in white robes, and palm branches *were* in their hands; and they cry out with a loud voice, saying, "Salvation to our God who sits on the throne, and to the Lamb." And all the angels were standing around the throne and around the elders and the four living creatures; and they fell on their faces before the throne and worshiped God, saying, "Amen, blessing and glory and wisdom and thanksgiving and honor and power and might, be to our God forever and ever. Amen. Then one of the elders answered, saying to me, "These who are clothed in the white robes, who are they, and where have they come from? I said to him, "My lord, you know." And he said to me, "These are the ones who come out of the great tribulation, and they have washed their robes and made them white in the blood of the Lamb. For this reason, they are before the throne of God; and they serve Him day and night in His temple ; and He who sits on the throne will spread His tabernacle over them. They will hunger no longer, nor thirst anymore; nor will the sun beat down on them, nor any heat; for the Lamb in the center of the throne will be their shepherd, and will guide them to springs of the water of life; and God will wipe every tear from their eyes." (Revelation 7:9-17)

But woe to those who are left behind, for they have refused the blood of the Lamb. Thus they shall be judged by the vengeance of the Lion. "Then I looked, and I heard an eagle flying in midheaven, saying with a

17

loud voice, "Woe, woe, woe to those who dwell on the earth, because of the remaining blasts of the trumpet of the three angels who are about to sound!" (Revelation 8:13)

And many Muslims will choose to follow the false prophet. For as we shall see, Mohammad was not God's servant, but a liar and false prophet. And his words were not of prophecy, for prophecy means to know the will of God. But Mohammad did not know the will of God, for his words were a product of Satan's will. "But know this first of all, that no prophecy of Scripture is a matter of one's own interpretation, for no prophecy was ever made by an act of human will, but men moved by the Holy Spirit spoke from God." (2 Peter 1:20-21) And at the end, Mohammad shall be thrown into the lake of fire. "And the beast was seized, and with him the *false prophet* who performed the signs in his presence, by which he deceived those who had received the mark of the beast and those who worshiped his image; these two were thrown alive into the lake of fire which burns with brimstone." (Revelation 19:20) And his followers shall be slain by the sword of the Lamb, and the beasts of the earth shall devour their flesh. "And the rest were killed with the sword which came from the mouth of Him who sat on the horse, and all the birds were filled with their flesh." (Revelation 19:21)

Introduction to Islamic "Truths"

Dr. Samuel Samson

These four Islamic truths will refute and discredit the Islamic faith in every street, city and country. And any intelligent and reasonable Muslim should study these truths carefully, that he might make a wise decision regarding his faith, and ultimately be delivered from the fire of judgment. And they can do this by accepting the truth which can only found through the Lord Jesus Christ of the Holy Bible. They should also understand that although the Christians have many times the number of Muslims in the world, they have no wish to rape, kill, or destroy other people, as the Muslims are doing. For if Jews, Christians and others non-Muslims, whom Islam has declared to be infidels, were to participate in the same atrocities, what would happen to this world? And if Christians were to impose Christian laws into Islamic countries, just as the Muslims wish to impose their pagan Sharia law into Christian countries, what would happen?

There are presently more than 1200 mosques in America, which truly is a testament of the love, humanity and harmony which exists in the United States. Yet the Muslims claim that they are peaceful people and wish to live in harmony with the rest of the world. But if this were true, then the Muslims would be offering other religions the opportunity to build their

19

churches and temples within their countries. And if Muslims were to allow this, then the world would view Islam is a peaceful religion. However, they refuse to do so, and their wicked intents are blatantly obvious to the rest of the world.

The facts to be presented here are both revealing and irrefutable truths. And the intent of discussing them is that all men may know that salvation does not come through Islam or Allah. For salvation can only come from the Lord Jesus Christ of the Holy Bible. For He is the only Savior of the world.

Allah is not God

Dr. Samuel Samson

Why is Allah, the God of Muslims, not Yahweh (Jehovah), the Biblical God of Jews and Christians? Who is the true Creator of the universe? Who is the living God, and who is an idol god? Which God should be followed and worshipped? Which is a god of evil and darkness? All of the above questions can be summarized by one simple question: who is the real God and who is the fake god?

We will first examine the truth and facts from the Quran, as the Quran gives reference to the Holy Bible. For from these references we can know the truth. The Muslims claim that the Quran is a divine book, and that it is the last book to be revealed to Mohammad by Allah, and that there is no other holy book to come after their holy book. And if it is true that the Quran is the last book, then Muslims must accept what their holy book says about the Holy Bible. Therefore, let us examine what the Quran brings to the table.

> 1. The Quran confirms that the prior scriptures of the Torah/Law of Moses, the Zabur/Psalms of David, and the New Testament of the Christians are all true and holy scriptures. (Quran Surat 1:5-6. 2:41, 2:89, 2:91, 2:201, 2:136, 3:3, 5:46,48, 6:92, 10:37, 46:30)

2. The Quran confirms that the Injeel or the New Testament is both Guidance and Light. (Quran Surat 5:46)

3. The Quran also confirms that the Torah of Moses is both Guidance and Light. (Quran Surat 6:92)

4. The Quran states that David was given the Zabur or Psalms. (Quran Surat 17:55)

5. The Gospel of the Islamic Essa (Jesus) is separate from the Christian Gospel. Yet no person has ever seen this Islamic book. This strongly suggests that the Muslims have been lying about this book's existence for the past fourteen hundred years. For there is no Islamic gospel about the Islamic Essa. (Quran Surat 57:27)

Therefore the Quran, the holy book of Muslims confirms that the Holy Bible is Truth, Guidance and Light. And the Quran as the Islamic source of authority, irrefutably supports the truth of the Holy Bible, that God Yahweh revealed Himself through Jesus Christ the Son. This means that Mohammad and all Muslims must abide by their own book and its writings. Thus they are bound and held accountable to give absolute respect to the Holy Bible, and not to insult or disgrace its teachings about the God Jehovah and Jesus Christ.

In brief summary as to Jehovah of the Bible, the God of the holy Bible is the God of all gods. (Deuteronomy 10:17) He is the First and the Last. (Isaiah 41:3, 44:6, 48:12) He is Omnipresent. (Psalms 139:7, Jeremiah 23:12) He is Omnipotent. (Genesis. 17:1, Exodus 6:3) He is Omniscient. (Psalms 39:1-6, Proverb. 5:21)

1. The God of the Bible is the one true living God. He created the whole universe through the Father. (John 1:1-3, Colossian 1:14-19) And revealed Himself through the Son (John 1:1, 14, 18)

2. The Holy Bible has been in existence before, and not after Islam. And the God of the Holy Bible, of Jews and Christians, establishes both authority and authenticity on its own, and does not rely upon other deities, messengers or books in order to validate its truths. Yet other religions give reference and respect to the Holy Bible, in order to serve their own interests. However, if they give reference and respect to the Holy Bible but refuse to obey it, then in biblical terms, they are hypocrites!

3. The Bible is a solid, valid, and self sufficient source which supplies the spiritual needs and fulfillment of every believer. It does not need the support of a deaf and dumb idol like Allah. Nor does it require the assistance of his

messenger Mohammad, who is both a liar and a false prophet who takes credit for doing nothing except seducing, misleading, and confusing the common people, and leading them into the fire of judgment.

Furthermore, Allah of the Quran commanded Mohammad and his followers to interact peacefully with the people of the Scriptures. (Quran Surya 10:94) And this essentially meant not to insult them, argue with them, or fight with them. (Quran Surya 29:46)

Lastly, Allah of the Quran suggested that the Jews, and especially the Christians, should do the following: "let the People of the Gospel judge by that which Allah hath revealed therein. Who so judgeth not by that which Allah hath revealed, such are evil-livers." Therefore we as Christians, should show them common courtesy by thanking this deaf and dumb idol of Allah for revealing to us the truth and the way. And at the same time we should not forget to ask this all important question:

O' Allah what do have to offer us that is better than our original, one, true God Jehovah? And are your blessings any better than those of Jesus Christ, if you can even give us a blessing?

Therefore, in light of the Quran's confession of the authenticity and authority of the Holy Bible, we come to the conclusion that God of the Holy Bible is the only one, true and living God, who revealed Himself through His Son Jesus Christ, the Savior of the world through the forgiveness of our sins.

And who is Allah?

We all know that there are many lords and many gods in the world, and that people are constantly worshipping them. But only Jews and Christians worship the one true and living God. (Psalms 96:5) And now we will highlight the facts of Mohammad's Allah, the God of Islam.

Remember, the Arabic word Allah refers to the Arabic god of a specific Quresh tribe/group. And to Muslims, it is absolutely certain that Allah does not refer to the Hebrew God Jehovah. *And all Christian believers must especially understand these differences, because of the serious implications and consequences of mistaking Allah as the same God as our Jehovah.*

Therefore why are they not the same God?

> 1. Mohammad never accepted nor followed the Jehovah God of the Jews and Christians. According to the introduction of the Quran by Pickthall, Mohammad never joined, followed, preached, nor promoted the Jehovah God of the Bible.
>
> 2. Mohammad joined the Hunafa (plural of Hanif), a group which turned away from the idol worship of that time period. The Hunafa were

25

the *agnostics* of that time period. They were not Muslims, and the word Islam had not yet been introduced to the world. Each Hanif sought truth through the light of his own consciousness. And Mohammad the son of Abdullah joined them. And here the question again arises, as to what sort of spiritual standard could the Hunafa have without a living God, without any divine revelation, and without any biblical prophets!

And why did Mohammad not continue the old religions of his forefathers (Abdul Mutlib, his grandfather, and Abu Talib, his uncle), which he had practiced during his first twenty five years? During that time period, there were 360 idols of Kabbah in Makkah that were chosen as gods by the Quresh tribes and other Arabic people. Mohammad was well acquainted with three of the worship groups. (Bukhari Vol. 3:2478. 5:4287, 6:4720)

a. His forefather's tribe believed and worshipped the idol Hubal, which was a statue that was eight yards in height. Mohammad worshipped this idol for the first twenty five years of his life.

b. The Manaf was another one of the 360 idols and Mohammad had a connection to this tribe as well. (Bukhari Vol. 4:2753, 3527)

c. Between the age of 25 and 40 years he joined the Hunafa group, the agnostics.

3. Allah was a common name used during this time period. And whenever a person by the name of Allah was made into an idol, at a later date the idol was named the Allah god.

4. Sometime, between the age of 25 and 40, Mohammad researched the background of his late father Abdullah's god and religion. And what was his father's god and religion?

He was part of the Hums tribe who worshipped their idol called Allah. And by worshipping Allah, his father's name and title became Abdullah. Thus when Mohammad researched the background of his father's religion, he found it originated with the Hums tribe. Mohammad felt comfortable with this idol Allah, and thus chose it to be his future god.

And this is the specific Islamic reference which proves that Allah originates from a false idol.

Narrated by Mohammad bin Jubair bin Mutim "My camel was lost and I went out to search of it on the Day of Arfa, and I saw the prophet (Mohammad) standing and I said to myself : *By Allah, he (Mohammad) is from the Hums. What brought him (Mohammad) here?*

And these are the notable points:

1. Not only one but two separate narrators have narrated the above Hadith.

2. They first thought that Mohammad was from the Hums tribe.

3. However, Mohammad was from the Quresh tribe, and his actual membership or affiliation was with the Hunafa, an agnostic group.

4. Mohammad was seen present at the sanctuary of Hums tribe.

5. The question came into the mind of the narrator: What brought him (Mohammad) here to the place of Hums? Did he come here to introduce himself? Did he want to preach to the Hums tribe? Or did he want to join Hums tribe? What was his motive? And nobody at that time knew Mohammad was affiliated with the Hunafa. And like his father, he came here to embrace the idol god Allah of the Hums. And eventually he would use this idol to introduce the idol god Allah to the whole world.

6. Another very important and interesting point is that the Quran and Muslims still claim that they all are Hanif, which is absolutely wrong. For the Hunafa were not Muslims, but agnostics. And Mohammad, the self proclaimed messenger, would introduce his amended Allah (the old idol god Allah of Hums and his new

future god) to the Arabs only, because Mohammad felt it was his responsibility to be a messenger for the Arabs.

8. When Mohammad's uncle Abu Talib, who had the same faith as his grandfather Abdul Mutlib, was on his death bed, Mohammad came to see him and invited him to join Islam. His uncle openly refused him and declared that he would remain with the faith of his forefathers. (Bukhari Vol. 6:4772)

Of special notation:

a. It was Abu Talib, the uncle of Mohammad, who raised Mohammad from childhood and supported him after the death of his father   and his grandfather.

b. Abu Talib was well informed about all of the 360 idol gods.

c. He knew that the idol god Allah of the Hums was not superior to his god.

d. Abu Talib and Mohammad were both idol worshippers of pagans in their own separate religious practices.

e. In light of these facts, and according to his Quran, Mohammad was the first true pagan infidel (Kaafir and Mushrik) born on the face of this earth. And thus so are his followers!

f. Another important fact is that the word *Abd* has two meanings: a) a male slave and b) a worshipper. Thus when attached with another word, such as Abd Allah or Abdullah, it means a worshipper of the Allah idol.

Therefore, Allah is the idol god of pagan Islam who appears in Quran Surat 109.

Whenever you read the Quran Surat 109, the first thing you should keep in mind is that:

1. Allah in Islam was the name of a man and not a god. Whenever the people of his time period turned this man Allah into an idol and began to worship it like the other 359 idols of Kabbah in Makkah, then Allah became a god.

2. Allah never created anything because he was not a true and living God.

3. The Muslims claim that Allah is the same God of Jews and Christians is absolutely false.

And more important references about Allah of the Quran:

1. He begeteth not nor was he begotten. (Quran Surat 112:3)

2. Allah was single and unmarried. How then could He have a son Essa when there was no consort or wife? (Quran Surat 6:102)

30

3. At a certain point according to Quran Surat 53:18-20, Allah had three daughters named Lat, Uzza and Mannat. This would also imply that Allah was married, yet he was not.

4. Allah did not have the virility nor the energy to produce a single son. That is why Muslims for the past fourteen centuries have opposed the true Holy Bible of Christians. For as we know "in the beginning was the Word and Word was with God and the Word of God. And the Word was made flesh, and dwelt among us, and we beheld his glory, the glory of the only begotten of the Father, full of grace and truth." (John 1:1-2)

It was only Mohammad who ascribed the qualities of a biblical God to Allah, and brought him to this supreme level. (Bukhari Vol. 6:4628)

And these aspects of Allah should be noted:

1. The Allah of Islam is of "time". (Quran Surat 79:44, Bukhari Vol. 8:6181-82) Allah is of time because he is an idol, and thus is not eternal, but is limited by time.

2. Allah was discriminatory. He gave wives and children to other prophets, but not to the Quranic Yahya (John) or the Quranic Essa (Jesus). (Quran Surat 13:38)

3. Allah respected only Islam and not the other religions, including Judaism and Christianity. (Quran Surat 3:85, 5:3)

4. Allah does not love sinners. (Quran Surat 2:190, 3:31) Yet the Biblical God Jehovah loves all people.

5. And according to Mohammad and Islam, only Allah can answer the following five questions:

a. What will happen tomorrow?
Answer: Mohammad and his followers lived in a time of ignorance. They did not have a calendar, and they did not make future plans.

b. When and where will a person die?
Answer: Just ask a suicide bomber and he can tell you the month, date, time and even the place where he will die.

c. What profits will be earned from a business?
Answer: Ask a banker, economist, or any business man and they can give you an accurate estimated profit, even in a bad economy.

d. When will it rain?
Answer: Any weather forecast person (on the TV, radio, or newspaper) can tell you when it will rain.

e. What is the sex of an infant in the womb?
Answer: Technology is so advanced that any

health clinic can determine what the sex of an infant is in the womb.

Therefore, remember these two important references in order to refute Islam anywhere in the world.

1. Bukhari Vol. 2:1664-1665

2. Bukhari Vol. 3:1360, 6:4772

In light of these irrefutable proofs, referenced from the most respected of Islamic sources, any person can conclude that the Allah of Islam is a deaf and dumb idol created by Mohammad for Mohammad. And Mohammad promoted this Allah from the beginning with money, violence, and power. And his followers continue to do so to this day.

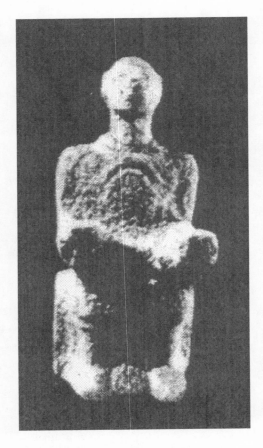

The idol god Allah of the Hums tribe

Why Mohammad is the False Prophet

Dr. Samuel Samson

We do not intend to insult or disgrace Islam by proving that Mohammad was a liar and a false prophet. But we will irrefutably clarify, with concrete facts, truths and proofs from Islamic sources, that Mohammad was a liar and a false prophet. ***And we apologize in advance for this clarification, but under the Biblical law it is our duty to clarify these issues***. For we do not want our Muslim brothers and sisters, and the coming generation to go through the fire of judgment. Thus, we will answer this question briefly and to the point.

Mohammad is a proven and declared liar based upon the Islamic holy scriptures of the Quran and Hadith. And these are the illustrated reasons why:

> 1. Mohammad wrongfully chose to worship the idol god Allah. This was the standard of his choice. For instead of worshipping and following the true and living God of the Jews and Christians, he first chose to follow the Hunafa agnostics. Following this, he abandoned them and worshipped the idol god Allah of the Hums, one of 360 idols of Kabbah in Makkah prior to the invention of Islam. (Bukhari Vol. 2:1664-1665) The idol god Allah which Mohammad chose to secretly worship and

preach about became his future god. Yet Mohammad never informed his followers that Allah was the idol god of the Hums. *Instead, he attempted to conceal this truth, which is now regarded as one of the biggest lies in the Islamic faith. And any liar like Mohammad who claims to be a prophet is considered to be a <u>false prophet</u>.*

2.   Mohammad's collective choice was to worship the idol god Allah, and not to befriend the Jews and Christians. (Quran Surat 5:51, 3:28) This would become his foremost crime of hatred!

Mohammad is also a proven liar and false prophet because it was not Allah who revealed these notions to Mohammad. For Allah was not a true and living god. And Allah was not the name of a god, but the name of a common man from this time period. Thus, Allah was an idol god created by the people, and accepted as an idol god by the Hums tribe. (Bukhari Vol. 2:1664-65) And an idol does not have the capacity nor the power to create and reveal divine truths to any man. But Satan and his seducing spirit does have the ability to put these thoughts into the mind of Mohammad, in order to accomplish his evil plans. (Quran Surat 26:221-222)

And the absence of friendship within a community or nation suggests that there is a presence of enmity and hatred within Mohammad's heart and mind.

3. Satan is a liar and is the father of all lies. (John 8:44) At a certain point Satan was so impressed by Mohammad's idolatry and lies that even he became a Muslim! (Mishkawt in Urdu Vol. 2:3179) And the Islamic scriptures give us a clear picture that Mohammad was able to convert Satan to Islam, which means that Satan is now an active member of Islam. And because Satan is the father of all lies, Islam does not have any problem in telling, inventing, introducing, and producing as many lies as it needs in order to accomplish their mission. And this is exactly what Mohammad taught them to do. (Bukhari Vol. 3:2692, Mishkawt in Urdu Vol. 2:4810)

And the jinns or demons loved fornicating with the liars and false prophets, because both enjoyed propagating lies. Thus the Jinns heard the Quran and also became Muslims. (Bukhari Vol. 6:4714) And as per the Islamic scriptures, because Satan became a Muslim through Mohammad, then both he and Mohammad would enjoy doing the same evil deeds.

Thus according to the best references of the Islamic faith, Mohammad is proven to be both a liar and a false prophet.

And what of the character of Mohammad? These are the references on the character of Mohammad:

> 1. Mohammad is considered to be a model prophet of Islam. "And lo! Thou art of a tremendous nature." (Quran Surat 68:4) But without any remarkable achievements, such a comment must obviously come from an illiterate source. For only Islam would admire such a common man without any justifiable reason.

> 2. Mohammad does not love mankind, but rather is a formidable enemy of humanity, as proven by this one monumental mistake: Mohammad would later confess and express remorse for his inventing of Allah and the Islamic faith. (Bukhari Vol. 8:6804) And due to this grave error of judgment, many Muslims will suffer through the fire of judgment. His false teachings, false hopes, and false promises to his followers will take a huge toll on humanity, because no one knows what will happen to them following their painful deaths. Even the leader of the Islamic faith Mohammad did not know what would happen to himself following his

death. (Quran Surat 46:9) (Bukhari Vol.   9:
7003-7004, 7018)

3. Mohammad ascribed many attributes and
qualities of the biblical Jehovah to his idol god
Allah and made him supreme like Jehovah with
the attributes of being a creator, a sustainer,
divine and merciful. (Bukhari Vol. 6:4474,
4628, footnotes, Vol. 9:p-302)

*But by Mohammad 's character, according to his own
teachings, he became the first and foremost Mushrik,
infidel (Kaafir), liar and false prophet.*

And these are just some of Mohammad's false promises
and teachings:

1. Do the opposite of what God requires of
Jews and Christians. (Bukhari Vol. 4:3462,
7:5892,99)

2. Impose and enforce Islam upon everybody.
Mohammad ordered his followers to keep
fighting and killing until their captives say La
Ilaha ilallah wa anna Mohammad Rasual Allah.
(There is no god but Allah, and Mohammad is
his messenger) (Bukhari Vol. 1:25, 2:1399)

3. Polygamy is moral and legal. One Muslim
could marry up to four wives. (Quran Surat 4:3)
And in fact, Mohammad violated his holy

book and married eleven wives. (Bukhari Vol. 1:268)

4. Only liars and infidels would do these inhumane and incestuous deeds:

a. Pedophile. Yet Mohammad married one of his wives Aishah when she was only 6 years old. Mohammad was 54 years old when he violated her at the age of 9 years. (Bukhari Vol. 7:5133-5134)

b. Daughter incest. Yet Mohammad violated Zaid (his adopted son) and his wife Zainab, the daughter-in-law of Mohammad. For he would marry his daughter in law, and granted himself an incestuous exception that was allowed by Allah and the Quran. (Quran Surat 33:37) (Bukhari Vol.9:7420)

c. Adultery of a neighbor's wife. Yet, one of his companions Dihya asked for a slave girl's hand in marriage. Mohammad gave her to him, but when he saw that she was very beautiful, Mohammad demanded her back for himself. (Bukhari Vol. 1:371)

5. Mohammad claimed that only 70,000 to 700,000 would enter paradise. (Bukhari Vol. 7:5811) Yet in Quran Surat 46:9, Mohammad confessed that he did not know what would

40

happen to himself following his death. Thus it was obviously a false promise.

6. Mohammad claimed that he could speak to Allah as an intercessor and bring his followers to paradise on the Day of Judgment. (Bukhari Vol. 6:4712, 9:7440)(Quran Surat 46:9,9:7003) Dear Muslim brothers and sisters, this will never happen. Do not become entrapped by his false promises and claims, because he is dragging you to the fire of judgment with himself and Satan.

7. A magic-affected person could be a true prophet, and Mohammad claimed that he was a magic-affected prophet. (Bukhari Vol. 8:6391)

8. Mohammad claimed that he had the seal of a prophet. (Quran Surat 33:40) Yet he never had the seal of prophet placed on him.

9. Mohammad used foul and abusive language, the characteristics of a liar and false prophet. For example, Mohammad instructed that if a follower wished to return to the pre-Islamic period then he must insert the penis of his father into his mouth. (Mishkawt in Urdu Vol 2:4683) Yet, if any other person were to say the same thing, he would be considered an infidel. Therefore, Mohammad was also an infidel and pagan. (Hadith Bukhari No. 1472)

10. Mohammad was an adulterer, which is the quality of a liar and false prophet. (Bukhari Vol. 3:3047-49, 7:5261, 5265, 8:6084)

11. One of the best references, comes from his most beloved wife and confidante, Aishah. (Bukhari Vol. 1:126) And Aishah said, "If anybody say that Mohammad has seen his Allah he is a liar." (Bukhari Vol 9:7380) To prove her statement she quoted from Quran Surat 6:104 (M. Pickthall) Mohammad also said "I have not seen the unseen" (Quran Surat 6:50) This all means that all Imaams, Muftees, Alamaas, and Muslim debaters, who claim that Mohammad ascended to heaven from the Dome of the Rock in Jerusalem and received five prayers from Allah with the assistance of the prophet Moses are liars as well.

12. Mohammad lied to everybody except his closest relatives, especially his daughter Fatima. And Mohammad said to Fatima that I will not be able to protect or save you from Allah on the day of judgment, but you will have to save yourself. (Bukhari Vol. 4:2753, 3527, 6:4771)

And there remain many more references which are defamatory to Mohammad's character, and prove him to be a liar and a false prophet. My request to the reader is that you share these facts with your Muslim brothers and sisters. And it is advised that you have a Quran at hand, in order to validate these references, so that the other party may not discredit these truths. May God bless you in your preaching with this irrefutable information at hand. However, remember to treat your Muslim brothers and sisters with respect. This material is intended to clarify these issues with the truth, and is not intended to insult anybody.

Why the Quran is a False Book

Dr. Samuel Samson

We have proven that Allah is not a true and living God. For Allah was the name of a man and an idol, like the other 359 idols of Kabbah in Makkah. When the people began worshipping the Allah idol, then it became the established god of the Hums tribe. We have also proven that Mohammad was a liar and a false prophet.

And what about the Quran?

> 1. Because Allah is not a true god, but an idol, then it is assumed that the Quran is a false book.

> 2. Because Mohammad is a liar and a false prophet, according to Islamic sources, then the position of the Quran becomes a falsehood.

> 3. Because the main source of the Quran is Allah, and its writer is Mohammad, a liar and a false prophet, then the Quran's authenticity and authority are automatically discredited.

And other references, which prove that the Quran is false, are as follows:

1. The Quran was a secret premeditated project of Mohammad's, as highlighted by Abu Hurairah. (Bukhari Vol. 1:118, 1:120)

2. Mohammad opposed Jews and Christians, and did not follow the teachings of the Holy Bible. Rather he began introducing his new book called the Quran to the Arabs. (Bukhari Vol. 42:13, :3462, Quran Surat 7:5892, 9:7362, 7542)

3. The descendants of Ishmael did not have any prophets nor a divine book. (Quran Surat 34:44)

4. Mohammad was instructed in the Quran to follow the previous prophets, but failed to do so. (Quran Surat 6:90-92)

5. Mohammad was instructed not to go against the teachings of Judaism and Christianity, but proceeded to do so.   (Quran Surat 42:13)

Was the Quran available at the time of Mohammad in a complete book? The answer is yes and no.

Why was the Quran not available as a complete book?

1. As we stated at the beginning of this chapter, because there is no true living God in Islam

then there could not be a true Quran or a divine book in Islam.

2. And in Mohammad's case, because he was a proven liar and a false prophet, then the Quran must be a false book.

3. And Allah said to Mohammad:

"Lo! Upon Us (rests) the putting together thereof and the reading thereof." Which essentially means, that it was upon Allah and Mohammad to put the Quran together and read it. (Quran Surat 75:17)

The question arises that because Allah was not a true and living God, but was a man with the name of Allah, who was created into one of the 360 idols, then who said this? It becomes a logical assumption, that all of this was a false lie from Mohammad, because Allah, the man and the idol, were dead, and Mohammad remained alive. For he wanted to promote the idol Allah, of his father Abdullah and the Hums tribe. And at the same time, Mohammad wanted to create an all powerful and living god. Thus, Mohammad introduced Allah as a living God, and ascribed the whole revelation of the Quran, as the holy book that Allah revealed to him.

4. Zaid bin Thabit, the scribe of Mohammad, clarified the issue in this way:

After the death of Mohammad, when Abu Bakr became the first caliph of Muslims, he along with Umar, the proceeding caliph, came to Zaid bin Thabit and ordered him to gather the Quran, because there was another contemporary prophet by the name Muslaima Kazaab, whom the Muslims were battling. Many Muslims, who learned the Quran by memory, were being killed, and there was a risk that if more Muslims were killed, then the Quran would be lost forever. And Zaid bin Thabit responded to Abu Bakr and Umar:

"How can you dare to do that which Mohammad did not do." (Bukhari Vol. 6:4986)

5. This is another Islamic scripture which irrefutably proves, that the Quran did not exist at the time of Allah. Narrated by Anas (bin Malik):

"When the Prophet died, none had collected the Quran but four persons: 1. Abu ad-Darda, 2. Muadh bin Jabal. 3. Zaid bin Thabit. 4. Abu Zaid. We were the inheritors (of Abu Zaid) as he had no offspring. (Bukhari Vol. 6: 4999, p-432, 6:5004, p-433)

And why was the Quran available at the time of Mohammad?

1. The Quran was not available in 114 Surats as it is available now.

2. But it was available in "Mashaf", small tracts originating from different sources.

3. The evidence reveals that the collection of the Quran was completed by infidels (the Ansari people, helpers of Mohammad from his mother's side), because Mohammad did not trust his own Muslim followers. (The Criminals of Islam, by Shabir Ahmad, MD,   p. 46)

4. As per Sheeyas : "No one collected the Quran in its complete form but Ali and his descendants." (The Criminals of Islam, by Shabir Ahamad, p. 45)

5. The few tracts (Mashaf) of the Quran were available, but Mohammad failed to solve the issues of the Quran's interpretation, and left this decision to the people, by temporarily ordering them to stop reciting the Quran.

Narrated by Abdullah: "The Prophet said, *"Recite (and study) the Quran as long as you agree about its interpretation, but if you have any difference of opinion (as regards its interpretation and meaning) then you should stop reciting it. (for the time being)* (Bukhari Vol. 6:5060-61, 9:7364)

Although Mohammad failed to solve these issues, Allah states in the Quran that we have made the Quran easy for you to interpret. (Quran Surat 54:17,22,32,40) So the Quran was easy to interpret, but Mohammad failed to solve the problem of its interpretation. Why? Because he was an illiterate prophet of illiterate and ignorant people. (Bukhari Vol. 2:1354, 3:1913)

6. Muslims would fight on the interpretation of the Quran. (Bukhari Vol. 6:5062)

7. The Quran was revealed in seven different ways. (Bukhari Vol 4:3220, 6:4981)

8. There was also a contradiction and fight on the availability of the Quran. (Bukhari 1:114, 7:5660, 9:7366)

Thus, in its present form, the Quran has been tampered with, changed, and corrupted.

The following are direct references which clarify, why the Quran which Islam boasts about is a big lie:

1. Not only the Quran, but everything in Islam is changed, nothing is original. (Bukhari Vol. 1:529-30)

Narrated by Ghainlan: Anas said, *"I do not find things as it was (practiced) at the time of the Prophet."* (Bukhari Vol. 1:529)

Narrated by Az-Zuhri when he visited Anas bin Malik at Damascus and found him weeping, after asking him why he was weeping. He replied, *"I do not know anything which I used to know during the lifetime of Allah's Messenger except As-Salat (the prayer), and this Salat too is lost."*

2. The deaf and dumb idol Allah's statement and confession:

"O' Mohammad you do not know what your people have innovated in the religion." (Bukhari. Vol. 6:4740, 8:6526, 6582, 9:7049-7051)

3. Mohammad also said that if one makes a change in our religion, then it is not our religion. (Bukhari Vol. 3:2697)

4. But Mohammad also taught Muslims to tell, invent, introduce, and produce any lies, in order to accomplish their mission. And this

dishonest act, according to Allah, was not a sin. (Bukhari Vol. 3:2692)

So where do you stand Muslim brothers and sisters? Where is your boasting? Come, let us reason honestly with these truths and facts.

In conclusion, we have proven, from many different angles, and with irrefutable Islamic references, not only is Allah a fake god, and Mohammad a liar and false prophet, but the Quran, the holy and divine book of Islam, is a false book. And this book will remain a fake until the Day of Judgment. And then God shall destroy it in the fire.

Why Islamic Proselytizing is a Sign of the End

Dr. Samuel Samson

This question is related to our Biblical prophecy, and the following specific points need to be made:

Fact 1: Deceivers will come and deceive you

Islamic proselytizing, especially towards Christians, shall take place, and Christians who are not firm in their faith will accept their Islamic lies. And here are few significant highlights related to the end:

> 1. There will be false Christs: many false Christs and deceivers will come to confuse, mislead and seduce Christians. (Mathew 24:5)
>
> 2. Many false prophets will come, and false prophets shall deceive you. (Mathew 24:11)
>
> 3. Persecution will come from non-Christians (especially Muslims): "Then shall they deliver you up to be afflicted, and shall kill you: and ye shall be of all nations for my name's sake." (Mathew 24:9)
>
> 4. "Many (Christians) shall stumble and accept their religions." (Mathew 24:10)

5. They will claim to do God's service: "The time cometh , that whosoever killeth you will think that he doeth God service." (John 16:2)

6. A falling away from Christianity is guaranteed to happen before the final Day of Judgment. (2 Thessalonians 2:3)

And these are a few important points for consideration:

1. To Islam, every non-Muslim is an infidel or Kaffir.

What does that mean? It means that every Christian, Jew, Hindu, Sikh, agnostic, atheist, and worshipper of any other religion is an infidel.

2. The Christians have a special biblical bond with Jews, which is both solid and positive. The Quran confirms that Muslims do not want any friendship with Jews and Christians. (Quran Surat 5:51, 3:28)

3. When we all are considered infidels to Islam, then there is no possibility that any nation which is Muslim, can extend their friendship to Christians. Yet it is the Christians who have demonstrated to other societies how to

extend love, peace and harmony to other nations without any hatred, killing or bloodshed.

Fact 2: Who will be the main opponent of Christianity during the end times?

The Holy Bible is very clear about this as well.

1. All nations will be against Christianity. (Mathew 24:9)

2. The other nations may be against Christianity in beliefs, but they will not be inhumane like the Muslims are. Why not?

a. They hold some value for human life.

b. They will not kill people and enforce their religion upon others, as Islam encourages its followers to do. (Bukhari Vol. 1:25 and 2:1399)

c. The Christians do not have any significant problems with other religions, because they preach and practice their religion within a set of boundaries, and do not cross the limits of oppression and violence, as Muslims are doing.

Fact 3: The main opponent of Christianity is Islam.

Here are the biblical and historical facts of this opposition.

The main reason for Islam's opposition extends back to Hagar, the mother of Ishmael and maid servant of Sarah, the wife of Abraham. Sarah was not able to bear children, thus she offered Hagar to her husband Abraham, to bear a child. But when Hagar became pregnant, Sarah despised her. Sarah severely afflicted Hagar, and Hagar tried to escape to the forest. An angel met Hagar and told her to go back to Sarah. The angel also gave her the good news that she would bear a child and he would be named Ishmael. And here is the main biblical reference to Islam:

"And he will be a wild man, his hand will be every man, and every man's hand against him and he shall dwell in the presence of all his brethren." (Genesis 16:12)

Points to be noted:

1. Ishmael will be a wild man (in Urdu the translation is "wild donkey") which means that his actions would be wild, and his descendants would be violent like wild donkeys. And this is exactly what has happened, even to this age.

2.. Future perpetual enmity and opposition means there would be no peace at all.

3. Both hands would be against each other. Which means that brother would war against brother, tribe against tribe, nation against nation.

And Muslims correctly claim that Hagar is the mother of the Arabs. (Bukhari Vol. 4:3358,7:5084) And that Ishmael is their father. (The stories of prophet by Ibn Kathir p-166) And that Mohammad is their prophet.

Thus, it becomes very clear that only Islam has been hostile towards the whole human race. Yet other religions have been tolerant of Islam's intolerant nature. And Christians should rise and teach the Islamic minority how to live in love, peace and harmony.

And what does it means when Jesus said love your enemies? It means to share your blessings with them, especially when they are in dire need, such as being hungry and thirsty, or trapped in a difficult situation. Your timely help can change your enemy's wicked nature, and ultimately save his soul.

Also, at the time of Ishmael's birth and during his childhood, his God and Abraham's God, was the true Jehovah God. Yet he abandoned his true Jehovah God, and began worshipping idol gods when he married an Egyptian. And from Ishmael until Mohammad, and from Mohammad to the present, the descendants of Ishmael have worshipped an idol god.

But Christian love does not mean that when a wild man approaches you, you lie down like a lamb. Nor does it mean that you take up his idol gods. In that situation, you need a special plan in order to refute their lies. And these are the specific references that you should know:

1. The deaf and dumb idol Allah, was not a god in his time, but merely a man converted to an idol and added to the other 359 idols of Kabbah in Makkah (Bukhari Vol. 3:2478, 6:4720, 1:1360, 2:1664-1665, 3:2478, 4:3039, 6:4772)

2. Satan converted to Islam through Mohammad. (Mishkawt in Urdu Vol. 2:3179) And the Jinns or demons became Muslims as well. (Bukhari Vol. 6:4714)

3. Mohammad was a historical liar. Announced and declared by his most beloved Aishah, the confidante and youngest wife of Mohammad (Bukhari Vol. 9:7380) who confessed that Mohammad lied when he claimed that he ascended to heaven and received five prayers with the assistance of Moses. (Bukhari Vol. 4:3207, 5:3887, 9:7410, 7440) Another different statement of that ascension. (4:3342)

4. Mohammad promoted adultery (Bukhari Vol. 7:5261,5265, Mishkawt Vol. 3:3047-49)

5. Mohammad was a pedophile. (Bukhari Vol. 7:5133-34)

6. Mohammad was a cheater (Bukhari Vol 3:2468)

7. Mohammad used foul language. (Mishkawt Vol. 2:4683)

Fact 4: How will Muslims convert people to Islam?

1. By preaching their doctrine in a deceptive way in order to accomplish their goal. For Mohammad encouraged Muslims to tell, invent, introduce and produce any lies in order to accomplish their task. And Allah does not consider this to be a sin. (Bukhari Vol. 3:2692. Mishkawt in Urdu Vol. 2:4810)

2. Through the Jihad by killing Jews and Christians in order to reduce their population. And increasing the number of Islamic followers by converting them with death threats. Mohammad said, "I am ordered to keep on fighting till they say La ilaha illalallah wa anna Mohammad Rasul Allah (There is no god but Allah and Mohammad is his messenger).

3. Converting followers by offering bribes.

4. By offering money to single mothers to give Islamic names to their children.

5. By bringing pregnant Muslims women to the US and the West so that they can give birth to their children here, obtain double citizenships, and continue to increase the Islamic population.

6. Muslims also say that they cannot defeat Western society through war or scientific technology. But the easiest way to defeat them is by using the wombs of their women. And the Muslim countries are infamous for their inhumane treatment of women.

And how did Mohammad treat his women? He always wanted to add new women to his life. But they did not have any respect for Mohammad, and did whatever they wanted to satisfy themselves sexually. Narrated Aishah: "Had Allah's Messenger known what the women were doing, he would have forbidden them from going to the mosque as the women of bani Israel were forbidden." (Bukhari Vol. 1:869) Mohammad said that he had the power of 30 men and he could have sex with all his 11 wives at once. (Bukhari Vol. 1:268) But Mohammad could not stop his women from fulfilling their desires. He was not able to satisfy them due to his poverty, (Bukhari Vol. 8:6450-6459) and his lack of physical health and energy. (Mishkawt Vol. 2:5120)

Therefore, in light of the above irrefutable facts, one can understand why the Muslims will use any method in order to convert people to Islam. And these surely are signs of the end times.

But this world does not belong to an idol god Allah, nor to Satan, nor to the false prophet Mohammad. For this world belongs to Jesus Christ, the Savior of the world, the First and the Last, the Alpha and Omega, the King of kings and Lord of lords. For "these are the words of him who is holy and true, who holds the key of David. What he opens no one can shut, and what he shuts no one can open." (Revelation 3:7) Thus He is the master of all things, and He is coming soon to judge this world, so be prepared. Now is the time to accept Him as your personal Savior. For your refusal will lead you to the fire of judgment, but your acceptance can lead you to eternal peace and joy in the kingdom of heaven.

Made in the USA
Charleston, SC
21 April 2011